ART AND GEOLOGY: EXPRESSIVE ASPECTS OF THE DESERT

This is a Peregrine Smith Book
Copyright © 1986 by Gibbs M. Smith, Inc.

Published by Gibbs M. Smith, Inc.
P.O. Box 667, Layton, Utah 84041

Book design by J. Scott Knudsen

Printed and bound in Japan

90 89 88 87 86   5 4 3 2 1

FIRST EDITION

Front cover painting: *The Raven Flies*, by Rita Deanin Abbey
Photograph by Patrick Barteck

p. 87: *Canyon Echoes*, by Rita Deanin Abbey, courtesy Valley Bank of Nevada Fine Art Collection

Library of Congress Cataloging-in-Publication Data

Abbey, Rita Deanin.
  Art and geology : expressive aspects of the
  desert.

  "Peregrine Smith books."
  1. Deserts in art.   2. Visual perception.
I. Fiero, G. William.   II. Title.
N8217.D63A3 1986   704.9'436   85-27621
ISBN 0-87905-201-5

ART AND GEOLOGY

EXPRESSIVE ASPECTS OF THE DESERT

Rita Deanin Abbey and G. William Fiero
Foreword by Richard Shelton

➔P

GIBBS M. SMITH, INC.
PEREGRINE SMITH BOOKS

To canyons, ravens, and wrens

Acknowledgments

Paintings, relief structures, and poetry are by Rita Deanin Abbey. The paintings were photographed by Michael Meagher.

Photographs of the desert are by G. William Fiero.

Special thanks to Charles Lynford Adams, Robert Rock Belliveau, and especially Aaron Paul Abbey for their suggestions and generosity of time in reviewing *ART AND GEOLOGY: EXPRESSIVE ASPECTS OF THE DESERT.*

Contents

List of Illustrations

Foreword

When a visual artist such as Rita Deanin Abbey and a geologist such as G. William Fiero focus their combined aesthetic, technical, artistic, and scientific abilities on something as overpowering and elusive as the desert country of the American Southwest, the results can be exciting. In fact, in this case, they are.

That particular combination—artist, geologist, and desert—is by no means new. It was customary for the teams of the United States Geological Survey, as they worked in the arid Southwest under John Wesley Powell's guidance, to include at least one artist. One of these was the most obvious example of a team all by himself, the remarkable Clarence Edward Dutton—artist, geologist, and writer. His accomplishments in the field of "geological aesthetics" (Wallace Stegner's term) leave us in the awkward position of not knowing what to praise him for the most.

His accomplishments also remind us, if we need any reminding, that we have fallen, or plunged into an age of specialization. In order to deal with a universe expanding at an incredible rate, we have a tendency to rely more and more on specialists with narrow shafts of knowledge and skills. And while specialists are necessary in today's world, the tendency to depend upon them to the exclusion of all else is dangerous. Somebody must integrate and synthesize what we learn about ourselves and the world in order to prevent social, cultural, and even personal fragmentation.

While very loosely within the area of "geological aesthetics," this work by Abbey and Fiero cuts across many other lines as well, particularly contemporary visual art, theories of perception, and archetypal patterns. It is not so much about what is out there in the desert to be seen, as it is about how to see what is out there. And how what is out there can, consciously or sub-consciously, affect the contemporary artist's work.

Learning to distinguish between the kinds of plants, animals, reptiles, insects, geological formations, and other elements which go to make up any one of the deserts of the American Southwest is more than a lifetime job; and sometimes we become so caught up in the effort, just to distinguish things from one another, that we forget the rest of the job. We must also learn to see what these things have in common, those recurrent properties which create, out of great diversity, the harmony we sense in the desert as in, perhaps, no other kind of landscape.

I have been looking at the Southwest's most luxuriant desert—the Sonoran—for more than twenty-five years, trying to see it clearly and see it whole, and of course failing to do either. I have even had the audacity to write about it some, a dangerous thing to do since one's observations on such a subject, once they get into print, can be checked by the specialists and found to be inaccurate. (In an age of specialization, it is much safer for a poet to stick to his or her internal emotional states, which can be lied about with impunity.)

Looking back over everything I have written about the Sonoran Desert, it occurs to me that what I have been trying to do is put all the pieces together, somehow to suggest the general harmony of the desert by presenting a set of specifics. But which specifics are congenial with others in a particular poem, and why? Or should I, as some poets do, simply grab elements of the desert at random, given such an enormous range of choice, shove them into a poem and hope that some magic power will make the product work out as an artistic whole?

I wish *Art and Geology: Expressive Aspects of the Desert* had been available to me many years ago, but I am grateful that it is available now. It has helped me see the "patterns that control," patterns that control shape, color, line, and texture in the desert. It has helped to train and improve my perceptual abilities, and to give me an understanding of some of the physical principles behind the harmony I know is there.

Perhaps I will write better poems because of it. Perhaps I won't. But what is more important, I will have a better contact with something beautiful that I love, and be able to see it more completely. There are many other benefits to be obtained from books; but none, I think is more important.

Richard Shelton
Tucson, 1985

Introduction

All knowledge has its origins
in our perceptions.

LEONARDO DA VINCI

The way we look at objects and interpret images is rooted in our cultural conditioning and inherited through genetics. These conditions can limit our ability to develop broader aesthetic sensibilities.

Many people become visually complacent about their environment: they settle into habits of seeing and never attempt to challenge or probe beneath the surface of their experience. Other people, however, because of personal motivation or because of the nature of their professions, seek techniques to increase their visual awareness. Exploration of unfamiliar images and the search for new methods of interpreting familiar ones are catalysts for expanding our views and revitalizing our observational powers. The discoveries result in an enriched appreciation of nature and our relationship to it.

The artist and the scientist cultivate their observational skills and their imaginations so that they may perceive the interrelationship of form, structure, and space. New perceptions enhance communication and diminish the gaps between nature, art, and the sciences. Commonalities emerge. Paintings to an artist represent more than mundane objects, local colors, and geometric figures, just as landscapes to a geologist suggest more than their components of rocks, soils, and plants. Both represent and share the fundamentals of space, form, and process. The artistic and natural worlds stimulate humankind's psychological, emotional, and spiritual forces. Increased perception transforms the commonplace into a creative adventure.

We, the authors, coming from the fields of art and geology, have independently arrived at a common ground of communication, especially in the way we relate to desert environments, space, color, and form. Our exchange of ideas resulted in *Art and Geology: Expressive Aspects of the Desert*. This book juxtaposes contemporary paintings and relief structures with photographs of geological phenomena, not to demonstrate a superficial similarity, but to present the closeness of the creative visions and experiences of the artist and the scientist. The paintings were not based on the geological photographs; rather, the photographs were selected because of their strong correspondence to the completed works of art.

We hope the book will open new visual vistas and ways of relating to art, natural surroundings, and to one another.

Rita Deanin Abbey
G. William Fiero

SEEING ART AND NATURE

The aim of art is to present not the outward appearance of things, but their inward significance.

ARISTOTLE

An art image provokes responses and invites multiple interpretations. The structure of an image is sensed and intuitively understood without verbal explanation. Visual arts are languages unto themselves. How the component parts of each work interrelate determines mood and message, and reveals the sense of unity of the individual artist.

Although aesthetic canons have greatly differed throughout history, an underlying concern of the artist has been to arrive at a completeness—the work is "finished" when all the parts are resolved into a harmonious whole. This feeling of balance, of things "being right," can be achieved through the diverse compositional possibilities of symmetry and asymmetry, centering and randomness, simplicity and complexity. In some instances the conflict of opposition is welcomed because it challenges the artist's creativity and the viewer's ingenuity. Qualities and elements so far apart as to seem irreconcilable function to develop the dynamics of movement, and bring to two-dimensional space an illusion of unlimited depth.

The artist reconstructs the random vocabulary of verticals, horizontals, diagonals, planes, volumes, cubes, spheres, textures, darks, lights, patterns, and color into an order of vital relationships inextricably linked to the dynamics of life. No static surface representation can do this, for it lacks penetration into the deeper nature of being. The artist finds new ways to comment on the times in which he lives as he strives to be in harmony with the rhythm of the universe.

We know little about our earth. Our handicaps are so profound that we scarcely recognize them, so accustomed are we to our ignorance. Virtually all our sensing mechanisms are crude and scarcely used. Only the boldest stimuli penetrate our sensory screen and register into our cranial computer. Therein lies a paradox. Our eyes, evolved for the watery world of our ancestory, are ill-adapted to our subaerial existence. Primitive organs, water filled and lubricated, only dimly perceive the plethora of sights envisioned by such optical masters as dragonflies and eagles. The desert, antithesis to our fluid past, has such contrast of color, light, shading, and space that even our crude eyes are sensitized, and quickly the visual system is overloaded. Such enormity of space—such contrast of color and light—can only be found in the stark openness of the arid lands. Consequently, most of us reject that which stimulates us so. The space and boldness of pattern transform visual diversity into fear.

Geologically speaking, the earth appears solid. Planes and tabular bodies penetrate both the external surface and the interior depths. We, however, are surface dwellers. Surfaces to us are primarily two-dimensional. Geologists still have evolved only the most crude techniques to represent on paper the real three-dimensional space in which we live. This handicap is met by geologists in their introduction to geologic maps. Few really survive the experience. Overcome by the impossibility of changing dimensions, many despair of ever visualizing depth on a piece of paper and become biologists instead. Others cannot perceive the third dimension at all, and this handicap prevents them from ever sensing a larger reality than a plane. The survivors master the skill, rudimentary as it is, of seeing and experiencing "depth."

Geologic mapping is the essence of geology. Those who practice it look at an outcrop of desert rock and project the solid matter into forms and shapes that penetrate the earth and interpenetrate each other. The patterns and flow lines mingle and cross like dancers composed of puffs of smoke. As the earth compresses, folds, pulls open, and buries, solid rock becomes fluid. Mixed by the amalgam of time, nothing is solid—all is dynamic and flowing. What we incorrectly perceive as unyielding and rigid is only frozen in an instant of time. The real earth is in the middle of a terrestrial pirouette. Even the best of geologic maps reflect a strobe flash unreality. Nowhere is the cosmic dance more vividly depicted than in the barren space of the desert. Unfettered by living debris, the ribs and bones of the rock are laid bare. The writhing musculature of the earth—all the arteries, cells, and cartilage are exposed and immobilized in the intensity of the desert sun.

The artist is also involved in a translation of spatial experience. The picture plane is a two-dimensional space on which to build a living world of three dimensions. Any point or line upon the plane transforms it to a spatial field. The field can be manipulated to create degrees of depth from relative flatness to deep, Renaissance linear perspective. Color, line, and texture are the fundamentals that interact to build the visual plasticity and meaning of the composition.

The structuring of the composition most often begins with the familiar rectangle or square—the shape of the canvas itself. These shapes generally connect man with his constructions. The development of a grid similar to the skeletal frame of a building often underlies the structural division of the picture plane. In building the composition, innumerable positive and negative ambiguities arise which create tension and increase movement and depth. The geometry of space as a building principle also unites the artist with the three-dimensional aspects of nature. The artist can clarify and integrate the structural aspects of forms within their surrounding space and express a relationship to them. The frozen space of an image on canvas can assimilate the past into the present, arouse limitless dramas of emotion, and evoke an inner essence of order and equilibrium.

The circle is another fundamental compositional shape. It can define a basis for perpetual motion, symbolically becoming earth, sun, atoms. Mandalas are Buddhist and Hindu symbols of the universe based on the circle. Cohesion, adhesion, expansion, and contraction—the constant throbbing of a heart—can be seen in their concentric patterns. For Tibetans, Mandalas express an essential relationship to cosmic rhythms; they grow and change while remaining rooted in a vital center. The growth rings of a tree, the crystal design of a snowflake, the anatomy of the eye—all of these are systems of self-contained relationships and growth. To "see" is to stir this consciousness of origins, embrace a dream, feel the totality of one's experiences.

Sing freely of simplicity
And live to the pulse
Of harmony

CIMA DOME

In his creations, the artist interlocks and balances the elements of art. Gravity plays an important role in either the defiance or acquiescence in the relationships. Mass can be fractured and lifted, suspended in unity, somehow simultaneously frozen and propelled, while brilliant light incises its fissures and bulk.

Large masses of similar material are common in the natural world. The lithified crust of the earth fragments into discrete plates. Large granitic masses exposed to weathering at the ground surface divide into rounded forms.

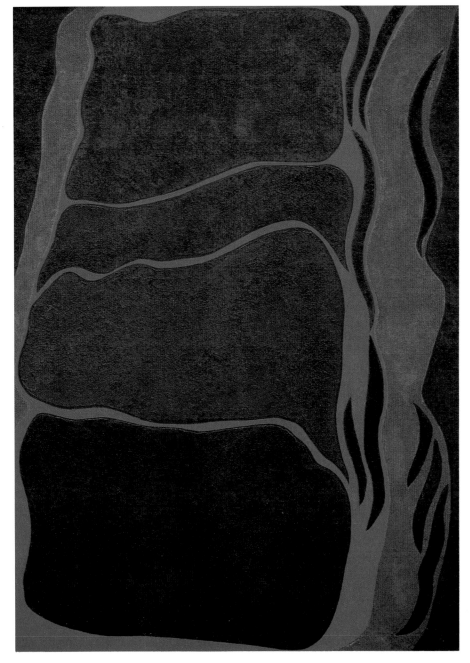

EXULTATION

BLEACHED CHOLLA

Noon sun bleaches a formerly vivid array of color. Forms can look isolated from their surroundings; silhouetted at dusk they reveal gnarled shapes with secret inner life.

Wood displays the meandering shapes often seen in nature. Rarely is the shortest route, the straight line, taken. Desert plants often appear twisted as though the force required for growth is preserved like a recoiled spring. During long periods of heat and drought, the stored energy sustains life. Living matter turns inward upon itself for sustenance and support.

DESERT HEAT

GUALALA

Overlapping planes create a wall or "aerial view" of interaction. Planes advance toward and recede from the viewer, leading him on a journey over mesas and canyons. Lines of color can suggest significant pauses, create momentum, and cause us to reevaluate position in space.

Erosion attacks weakness. Material will be divided along flaws which are often unseen. The force of moving water exploits a fracture or soft material, and soon rock, which appears to be uniform, is divided into isolated planes, masses, and shapes. Lumps, surfaces, or blocks of solid rock appear to melt into curved patterns that slowly move apart.

NASCENT SANDSTONE

SEVEN SISTERS

Vertical fractures in brittle rocks become planes of weakness as weathering and erosion attack rocks. Failure along these cracks results in vertical walls and angular junctions of the planes of the rock. Blocky masses of stone are left from the struggle of the primordial elements of disintegration. Cleavages widen to separate masses.

Pulsations are created pictorially if the forces of expansion are reversed to be seen as contractions. A continual metamorphosis can then occur in these lines.

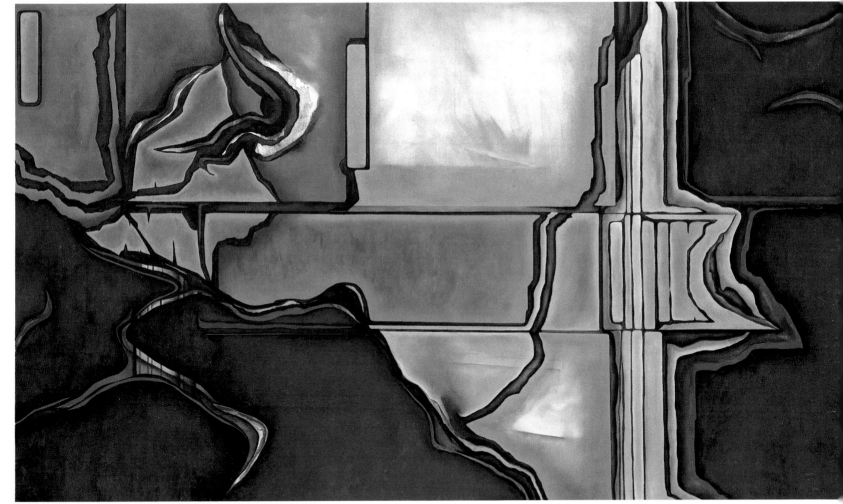

FISSION

SPRING MOUND

Spring water, charged with minerals, seeps through mud to the floor of an ancient desert. Slowly, layers of minerals deposit concentrically around the spring's orifice. The flaking shales break apart and expose the rind of nature's old plumbing.

Centrifugal rhythmic forces merge into Mandala form as if infused with fluid. Color merges with the movement, yet clearly attempts to seek momentary rest. The power of the movement, however, builds emotional momentum and maintains the memory of past watery channels.

WOMAN IN THE SURF

ELEMENTS AND IDEAS

I know quite certainly that I myself have no special talent. Curiosity, obsession, and dogged endurance, combined with self-criticism have brought me to my ideas.
ALBERT EINSTEIN

Our perception of desert regions, where space abounds, makes us conscious of the brevity of human life and, in contrast, of unending time. Such distinctions are inherent in this complex environment. For every humbling reaction brought on by the endless vistas of the desert there is a counter realization that we have the skills to develop a sense of its order and explore it in meaningful ways in the short time we are here.

Vast openness actually suggests concealment, secrets beyond sight inside ourselves, dark caves and mysterious, narrowing canyons that beckon exploration. It is in the immediate foreground we find tangible detail, layers of rich stratified colors—rocks that can be climbed, picked up, examined. Shrubs, cacti, mesas, and cliffs are encompassed in intelligible patterns. Then a quail or roadrunner scrambles from sight as a fleeting experience, and this momentarily isolated, smaller picture in turn provokes a spectrum of wonder, emotion, and thought. The specific and the eternal, the small and the grandiose, fluctuate in our sight and in our mind.

Duality as an intrinsic component of composition exists both pictorially and geologically.

For an artist, the plants, animals, rocks, and hills transform into visual elements of dark-light, surface textures, geometric and amorphous structures, colors, shapes—an array of contrasting images and suggestive interactions of space which intrigue, overpower, and precipitate creative ideas.

The geologist, studying the composition of the earth, is faced with a unique paradox. In order to understand the amazing array of detailed textures, lines, and colors, he must be able to comprehend the large-scale processes that created these particular characteristics. However, to differentiate which process is responsible, the geologist must integrate myriad rock details. Moving intellectually between the large and small scale, the geologist must experience a duality of vision and thought. Thus, the scientist viewing earth materials and the artist considering landscape and space arrive at the same point—a simultaneous viewing and conceptualizing of the microcosmic and macrocosmic worlds that surround us. Nowhere is this dichotomy of view more necessary or obvious than in the desert.

Life lies concealed beneath and within the desert rocks and soils. Lying dormant below the earth's surface are ancient seeds wrapped in a chemical coating. When excessive rain has washed away the germinating inhibitors, the warm sun arouses the first stirrings of growth and the seeds suddenly swell and burst into life. After tens, hundreds, or even thousands of years of dormancy, green plants push above the desert floor. Undeveloped life forms awaiting precise conditions are the bases of all biological beginnings. The unexpected emergence of unique fragrances, delicate petals, and rich patterns contrasted with rough, arid, monochromatic hard textures is an overwhelming juxtaposition of elements. These surprise relationships startle and delight the unsuspecting observer. From a seemingly lifeless soil, rebirth.

Rocks, the seeds of the earth, are pressed upward in timeless regeneration as well. Massive geologic forces stir within the thermal cauldron, which lies a scant distance below the desert floor. The land heaves upward in spasmodic releases of energy. Balancing this force, in a duet of seemingly frozen motion, is the great leveler, gravity. The earth, by its very mass and size, generates internal heat energy to deform and crumple its thin crust. This same mass accounts for the gravitational pressures which inexorably smooth surface irregularities. The western deserts of the United States with their great flows of internal heat and periods of extreme rainfall and aridity, focus in sharp contrast the forces of uplift and erosion. The interplay of these diametric energies is balanced and momentarily captured in geologic forms.

One sculptural example of enormous mass, height, and structure is precariously perched in a remote area of Arches National Monument near Moab, Utah. Delicate Arch frames a segment of the vista, making the view graspable and breathtaking. The human eye strives to achieve completion and comfort on its own terms, but an arch, or natural bridge or window, encloses and selects space without thought or visual strain. The frame, itself a result of motion and geologic process, alerts us to light-dark contrasts altered by the varied positions of the sun and reveals the nuances of the passage of the day. Standing under Delicate Arch, the viewer's perspective of mass awakens the reality of earth-human relationship.

The most active agent of erosion, even in the arid lands of the Southwest, is water. Occasional cloudbursts quickly fill the declivities, and rushing torrents of brown silt-laden water scour powerfully downward along any fracture or weakness of rock. Almost as abruptly as the flood begins, the waters recede and the downcutting ceases. Deep canyons and narrow recesses result from intermittent and catastrophic forces.

The cool inviting walls of canyons often shift mood and perspective. Enclosed in a canyon space, one can still feel the motion of water, the continuum of millions of years of action in the polished smooth and sensuous qualities of the forms. An arch requires one to look through the framed space at right angles to a distant vista. Being deep within a canyon provides a cathedral-like perspective toward a slice of intense sky. The light subtly sifts downward until it is broken by shadow, movement, and color in the rock.

The forces of erosion—chemical weathering and gravitational pull—exploit weaknesses in rock, creating cavities and releasing particles from the size of a molecule to multimegaton boulders. The difference of scale is perceptible only to small creatures, like humans, but seen within the context of the immensity of the earth, such size differential is insignificant—the process is the same.

Enclosed spaces such as recesses, caves, and overhangs result in space-frame variations that often dramatically present the effects of intense chiaroscuro: the interaction of light and dark. The dark, craggy, embryonic interiors of caves exaggerate the brilliance of exterior light; the juxtaposition is one of the most masterful contrasts in nature.

Geological deposition yields horizontal beds. The moving detritus of the earth— sliding, rolling, and flowing to the sea under the uncompromising pull of gravity—may be temporarily restrained by natural dams or lowland areas. In such places, sediments seek the angle of greatest repose and least work—the horizontal—as though foretelling their ultimate horizontal state in the deep seas. Vertical forces, responding to thermal instabilities within the earth, periodically move lithified ocean sediment upward, above the sea. Frozen into their transitory parallel layers, these newly exposed rocks are again in disequilibrium. Often tilted or bent by pressures of uplift, the disturbed parallel layers disrupt ultimate forms.

Sliced by fractures, the layers lie exposed to the disturbance of surface erosion once more. Giant walls are aesthetically seen as bas-relief structures and as murals which lend themselves to imaginative interpretations; they create shifting, sectional compositions as wide and high as vision allows us to encompass. The contrasts of stratified textures and stains exhibit nature's harmonic design differences. Such contrasts augment fantasy and curiosity, as well as geological reality.

The vast diversity of desert forms invites creative responses and unlimited appreciation. The aesthetic rewards one derives from the desert arouse a commitment to its preservation.

Awaiting the sun's urging
Clusters of cacti work slowly
Toward bloom

A route determined before our conception
Before the clutter of our possibilities
When only water separated the mountains
And trees kept the space from emptiness

Black

*Our inner universe has its suns,
moons and galaxies that intermingle
with darkness.*

NATHAN CABOT COLE
ABSTRACTION IN ART AND NATURE

Black lava rock derives its light absorption from the complete mixing of its component minerals. Molten rock, with all its elements in the finest possible state and thoroughly diffused, abruptly pours out on the cold land surface. The magma freezes almost instantly, and the elemental particles have insufficient time to organize. Thus, lava lacks crystals or internal differentiation. The result of the solidified diffusion is the fundamental color of the geological world—black.

The use of black as the lone color in a work of art emphasizes the significance of texture, light, and form. It also acts as a unifying force and conjures a multiplicity of meanings. Inner tensions from darkness come to life, pulsate, and enlarge under varied light conditions. Changing light also drastically alters form as it yields to surface contours.

Constituent materials determine texture as well as the qualities of light absorption and reflection. The interplay of light and texture offers a wide spectrum of rich graduated values and nuances within the one hue. The medium and the placement of forms in physical space determine the quality of blackness. How much of the light is absorbed and how much is given back with warm or cool casts of blue, green, brown, or red depend upon this quality of blackness. In an afterimage effect, after moments of fixed vision, black appears on our retina as white, which includes the total spectrum of color. Volcanic rock, so prevalent in desert regions, can become mirror-like and glow luminously white, as can a raven soaring in a canyon. The eye of the camera also reveals this negative afterimage effect.

Absorbent and reflective materials used in making works of art create extreme tensions of contrasting relationships. Because of the intrinsic characteristics of fiberglass, polyurethane foam, resin, wood, and plexiglass, textural differences are readily achieved which lend themselves to strong semblances of frozen motion. Polyurethane foam creates life-like forms which grow and take shape through thermal action. When solidified the form contains the process of this dynamic action just as lava does in nature. Forms that have cooled and stabilized through time contain evidence of their development in their final state. Fiberglass wrapped over underlying relief armatures complies to the contour surfaces of its supportive structure. Lava flows exhibit a wrapping aspect when a cooled or frozen exterior contains a still flowing molten interior.

When two different kinds of lava from two different time episodes are seen together, their opposing properties reveal the powers of time and contrasting movement caused by the internal fluid pressures. One form, with insufficient liquid, results in a tumbling action of the lava. The other form, with more liquid, flows in a continuous way. Each appears as different values of black with variable coloration.

These oppositional characteristics may temporarily prevent visual integration and may arouse contradictions in our thinking, yet they exist comfortably and harmoniously in nature and in inventive art compositions. The impact and communicative power of the image is dependent upon the reconciliation of contradictions. The image must combine and organize elements that the artist sees physically with those he senses emotionally, conceives intellectually, and strives spiritually to realize. Contrasting dynamic forces challenge and stimulate the creative imagination. The acceptance of contraposition as a basis for innovation and motivation presupposes awareness, receptivity, and readiness to explore new possibilities of integration. Nature, like some works of art, adds to our understanding of the roles of time, motion, and essence itself, thus moving us to larger perspectives of mental and visual balance.

Night, the widow of the universe,
Covering the flower and the stone
Devoted to seclusion
And freeing the soul, alone

LAVA TOES

Polyurethane foam and basaltic magma involve similar thermal actions and result in kinetic
forms that appear three-dimensional and reflect light from material that would otherwise
be absorbent.

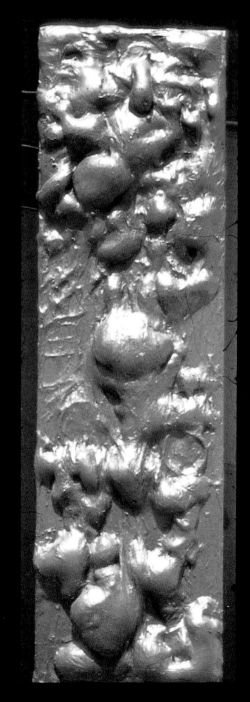

BAROQUE ALTAR

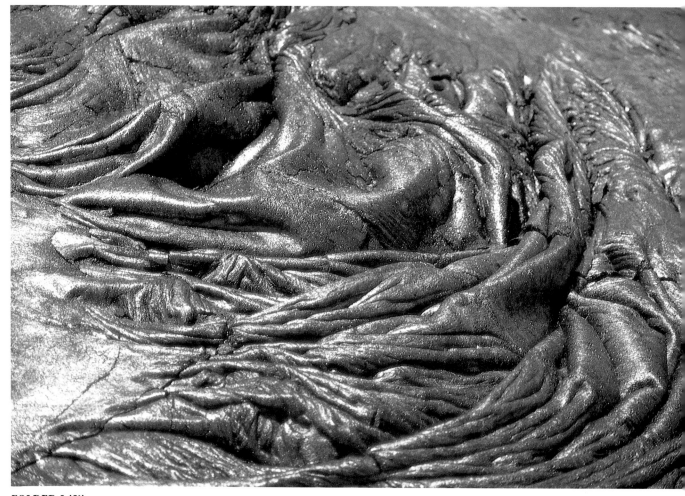

FOLDED LAVA

Matt and cloth fiberglass, saturated in polyester resin and wrapped over metal and wood armatures, and folded basalt from a recent laval flow, suggest an emergence of primal forces. Matter is momentarily frozen in time and space, and is perceived as permanent because the eyes that see it survive for only one instant.

PRIME MATTER

AA AND PAHOEHOE

Combining materials of different natures into flat and bulky forms and into rough-smooth textures that are both absorbent and reflective unites spatial levels in a tactile image. Observable physical differences may result from only minor variations in internal form. Slight chemical changes through time yield surface textures of great variety, even when the materials are derived from the same source.

POLARITY

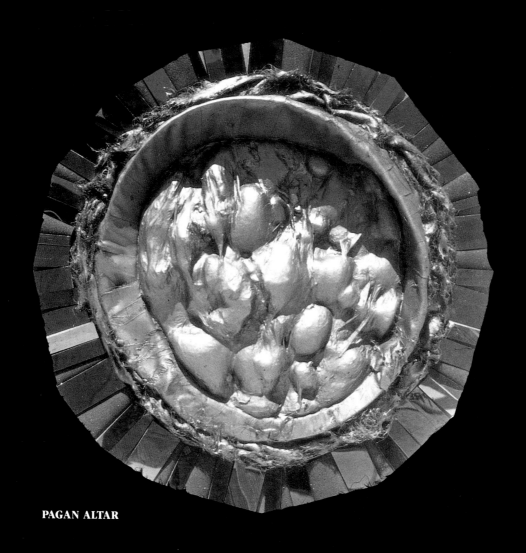

PAGAN ALTAR

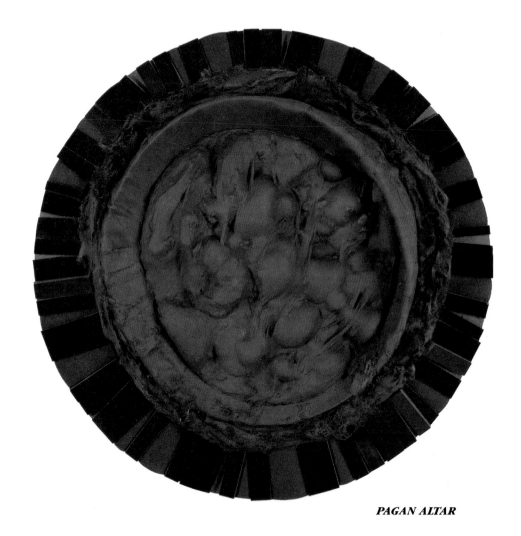

PAGAN ALTAR

When photographed, black often reveals white—its afterimage color. The film, acting like the retina of the eye, retains this visual phenomenon. Polar opposites, like Yin and Yang, are often only perceived images of the same nature seen from a different angle or with a seemingly insignificant internal or external variation.

Color

On my mountain top, then, two realities met: myself and a color.

JOSEPH WOOD KRUTCH
THE DESERT YEAR

The nature of light and color has always been of concern to the artist and the scientist. Mankind has utilized color for expressive, symbolic, psychological, mystical, and utilitarian purposes.

Detailed theories exist that assist the artist, designer, and manufacturer in understanding color systems. Color, especially for the painter, and most especially in the desert, is a means to explore, express, and energize intangible, nonverbal forces.

An understanding of color through a study of color relativity is antithetical to limited traditional theories, which have a tendency to restrict visual exploration. A system of color analysis that stresses the importance of the variability of vision emphasizes the uniqueness of changing viewpoints and of each individual's eye structure. Every color has its own personality, and some colors are seen as more dominant and stable than others. Through a trial and error approach, the spatial impact and importance of figure-ground (object and surrounding space) relationships emerge. The relative placement of one color to another alters its individuality, its pronouncement, its subtlety, and gives the illusion of changing its quantity and even its position in space. Color interaction creates tension, plasticity,

depth, and forces that often thrust beyond the boundaries of the conscious. The investigations into color by the poet Goethe, and the work and theories of color relativity by the painters Hans Hofmann and Josef Albers, opened new possibilities of "seeing" vitally with imagination and awareness, of exploring color as energy, and of enriching experience. Color perception ultimately remains a personal phenomenon.

The artist sees with his entire organism through a complex personal process. He feels, generates, and rearranges pigment into visual fields which he strives to structure with his sense of unity and harmony. Color is the artist's vehicle, his way of relating to, transcending, and inventing his world. With it he has an inexhaustible tool to create space, illusion, direction, and time. The artist learns from nature. Color shifts throughout the daily cycle, to create effects that fade, flatten, reveal, and deceive space and form. Light creates a continuum of infinite instrumentation where color exists for its own sake. The richness of contrasts ranges from dark to light, from silhouettes to three-dimensional depths. Dust particles reflect breathtaking spectral relationships. Climate, temperature, and haze also affect color experience. Every aspect of our surroundings and of ourselves conditions how we see.

Color in the desert reflects purpose. What might appear to an untrained eye to be random particles of color are not random at all. Desert colors reflect attempts to achieve stability and equilibrium within an environment of rapid change.

Few environments on earth achieve the extremes of the desert. Drought is followed by intense rainfall and flash floods. Daily changes in temperature often exceed fifty degrees. Periods of intense bleaching sunlight are followed by lingering multi-colored sunsets that sink into cool blackness. The rocks and living forms must adjust to these radical changes, and the use of color is one technique to achieve a stability.

Desert plants assume colors to change their reflectivity of the sun's heat. Light greens, white hairs, and shiny residues reflect the sun's rays, allowing plant tissue to survive in scorching temperatures. Pale greens in stems and trunks permit the food-producing photosynthesis to occur in all the surfaces of the plant and not just leaves. Brightly colored and aromatic flowers of spring attract the pollinators across the wide empty spaces between plants. The vital business of reproduction is aided by these visual stimuli. Plants are also sensitive to soil colors. Light soils, which reflect the sun's heat and remain cooler than surrounding dark soils, attract many species that find the warmer soil intolerable. Plants are not only producers of color, but are themselves color sensitive. Many light-colored desert soils are stabilized by lichens clinging to soil particles. Whole areas of dark soil, on close inspection, are revealed to be light soil covered with dark lichens. Forests of these microplants agglutinate soil fragments into lumps, and coat the desert floor with vegetation only a few millimeters high.

Rocks respond to their environment through chemical change. The variations of heat and moisture affect the chemistry of the rock, and these alterations result in color variations. Exposure to air causes changes in rock due to the contact with oxygen. Oxidation alters chemicals into new states as the rocks decay. Iron minerals become yellow and brown as rust forms. Light reflecting off layers of one-dimensional atomic structures causes pleochroisitic patterns of purples, blues, and dark reds to shine.

Increased exposure to surface geologic processes—such as rainfall, temperature changes, and oxidation—"ages" the rock. Lines and wrinkles form along planes of weakness and the softer parts are removed.

Concentrations of iron and manganese are leached out of the rock and soil by the solution of desert rains and are veneered on the rock surface by the intense heat of the sun's rays. The rock darkens through the development of the unique patina of the arid lands to produce a dark desert varnish.

The characteristic tones of the desert—brown, black, and pale green—result from adaptation. The changes in the desert plants and rocks to the shades of desert color are purposeful—equilibrium is achieved.

To the observer of the desert, this equilibrium prompts a recognition of tranquility. The desert appears to be a quiet environment of well-adjusted rocks and plants. All must fit into the pattern, or there will be no survivors.

I love red
It does not caress
Or lead one to guess
Its nature
Is never uncertain
Oh!
To be so unashamed

The ancient elements, fire and water, left their prints on the cliffs of desert sandstone. The blazing hot Mesozoic sun parched the ancient sand dunes, lithifying the sands into reddish rock. Today the forces of another desert tear open the old sand dunes. Lashing storms of wind and water expose the inner structure of the long ago desert.

Form and structure build the excitement of texture, color, and planes and create three-dimensional space. Torn edges are the result of elements acting upon one another. Vertical and horizontal variants stimulate energy forces and fuse color mixtures.

VALLEY OF FIRE

ELEMENTS

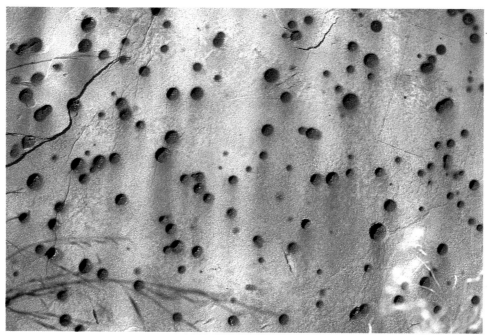

RED ROCK CANYON

Spherical concretions are formed by the cystallization of iron from ground water. The oxidizing iron nucleates around points within the rock, and the red rust stains the surrounding sandstone. Red spots freckle the rock's face.

The thin quality of paint runs down the canvas, staining and carrying transparent washes onto lower areas. The interplay of light from and on the canvas becomes atmospheric, stimulating afterimages, halos, and shadows, suggesting stained rock.

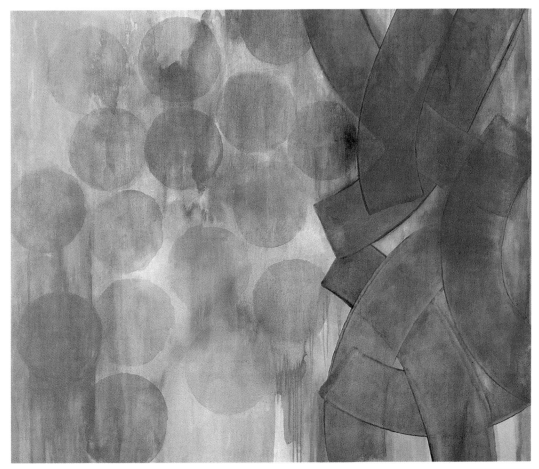

SUN SPOTS

CONCEPTION BAY

The clarity of desert sky and air combines with the vivid colors of sunrise and sunset to flood the landscape. In a land where sky and rocks dominate, brilliant hues blanket the desert with orange and black. Colors at dusk merge atmospheric remnants of the sun's intensity and penetrate all matter. Pinks, greens, yellows, and sky blues disappear from the spectrum leaving purples, oranges, and reds, fusing and melting from dusk into night.

DUSK

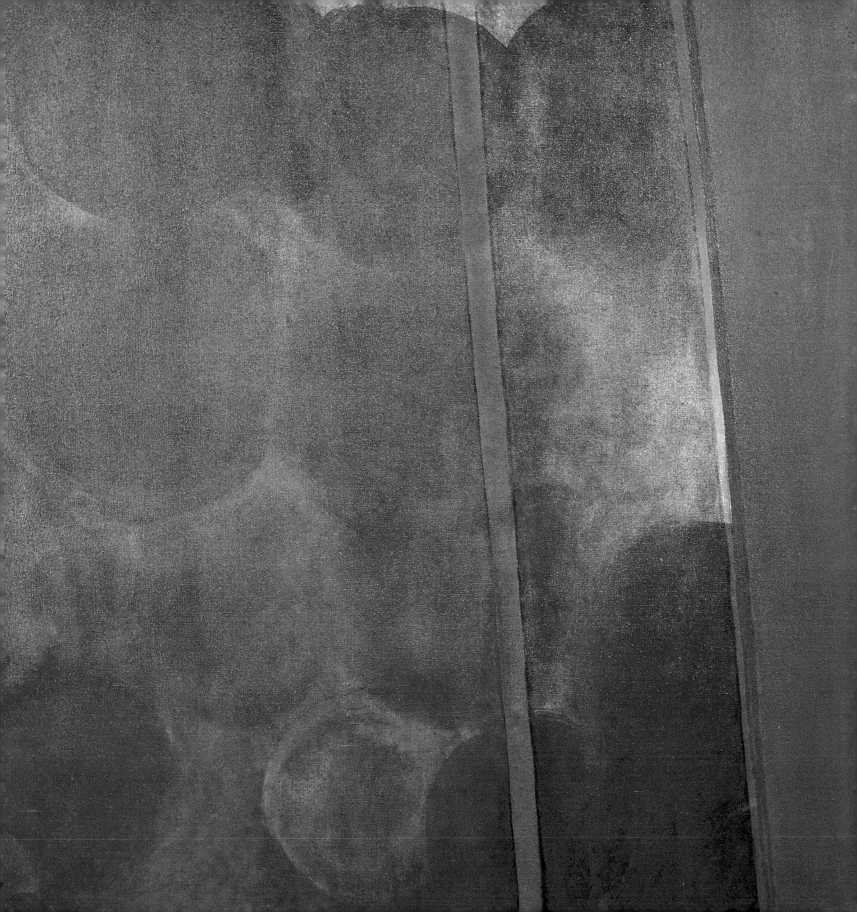

MONUMENT VALLEY

Long trails of moisture descend from massive clouds. Rain, in the desert, is a visual event. The cloud source, the falling virga of rain, and the impact on the earth are all clearly discerned. It is a land of open honesty. Subdued color emerges with moisture. A magical softness develops in the desert and edges blur. Dramatic spotlights often beam down through spreading clouds to electrify and emphasize a contrasting area set apart on the vast stage. Greys, terre verts, tints, and values of blues coexist with warmer wet browns, ochres, and sienna earth tones.

DESERT RAIN

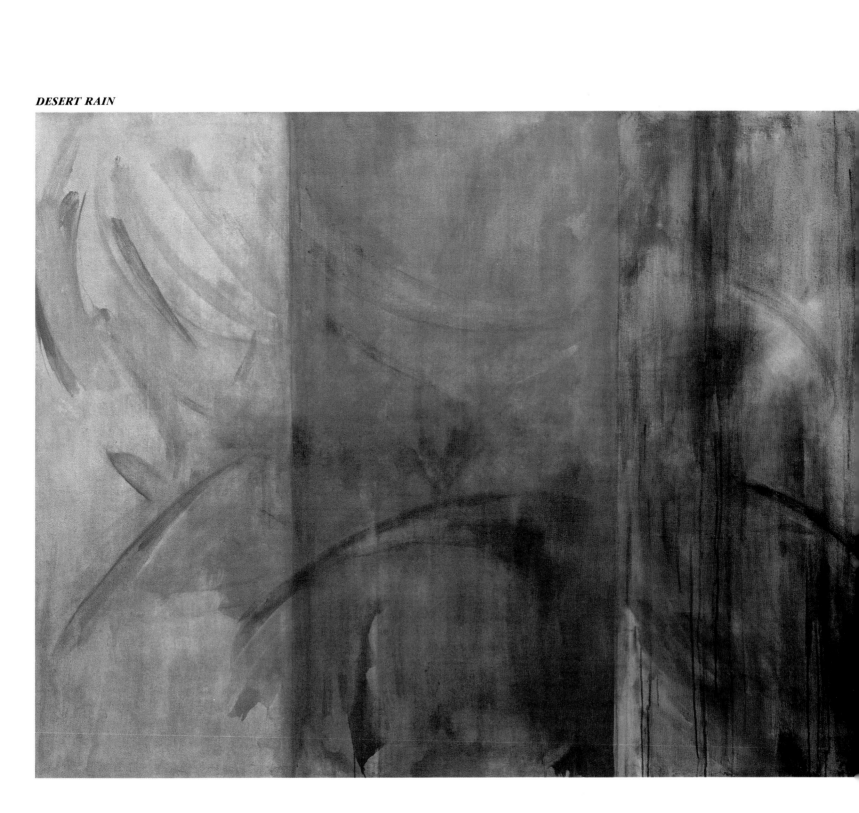

Line

. . . a weaver who has to direct and interweave a great many threads has no time to philosophize about it; he feels more how things go than he can explain it.

VINCENT VAN GOGH
FROM A LETTER TO HIS BROTHER THEO

Lines travel in various directions—diagonally, vertically, horizontally. Lines may be curved, straight, zig-zagged; they may be thick and dominant, thin and fragile. They may meander or scribble, repeat, fade into infinity, reappear as geometric or organic shapes that abstractly vanish again; they may clarify, divide, unify, or create grids. In a work of art, lines force the eye to explore surfaces and depths through movement, creating patterns of varied velocities. Successions of lines build energy and motion and seemingly accelerate time.

Lines are the equivalent of time for the geologist as well, so much so that many geologic sections contain features referred to as time lines. Successions of lines in nature are eternal rhythmic flows of repetitious seasonal cycles—wind action on sand, waves of water and time on earth—informing us of the history of matter and symbolically exposing an existing continuum.

For the artist, lines may be strokes or contours, imparting emotional, expressive, or intellectual qualities. Clusters of cross-hatching lines, dispersed or in directional groupings of close proximity, develop optical mixtures of light and dark that govern the three-dimensionality of form. Contour lines, flowing across topographic or geologic maps, visually represent height and depth.

Boundaries, geometric planes, solids, and symbols impart paths for discovery, wonder, and change.

The primordial, infinitely varied lines of the cranial suture joints are as distinct as the unique lines of the palm or the descriptive language of a signature. The vertical anatomic mid-line divides bilateral characteristics that describe balance, function, symmetric and asymmetric tendencies. The vertical or horizontal stripe in nature reveals an abutment of forces, as well as a preservation of environmental conditions. Lines guide our senses in our interpretation of the physical world. Canyons, cliffs, rivers and shores, all have lines that instruct our intellect and emotion. Without lines, patterns would not exist and the arrangements we perceive in our surroundings would fade. Lines serve to visually order our two- and three-dimensional worlds. They align our senses, expand our range of direction and perspective, and coil us into clockwise and counterclockwise helical systems.

Hondo canyon at night
Cold with frozen mysteries
No one could predict
The thawed hum of your stream
And friendship in the morning

CATARACT CANYON: GYPSUM STRIPE

Lines create directional forces. They emphasize and represent the collecting and dispersing of energy fields. They also create boundaries separating or uniting areas of space. These forces can be related to schisms in our emotional makeup, internal divisions that are preserved in our personality and behaviour. Time gives the appearance of being a linear dimension if studied within a short perspective. A brief but dramatic change in the geologic environment may create a linear feature such as this gypsum bed in the wall of Cataract Canyon.

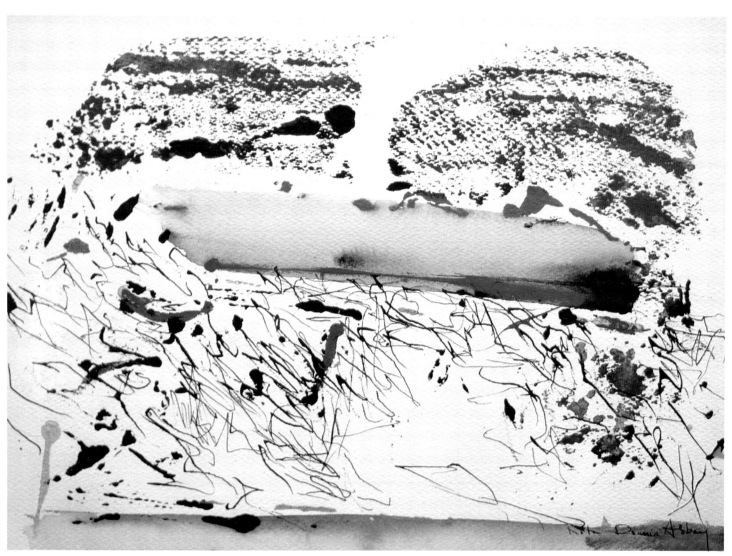

STRIPE - RIVERTRIP #9

WEST RIM, ZION

Line can exist as a positive space traveling over shapes. It can also be viewed as a negative division that determines mass areas on both of its sides, defining characteristic contours or shapes along the edges of these masses. Forces of erosion scribe the land with curvilinear patterns. Curved lines often enclose areas of differing energy. Glaciers flowing down mountain flanks, winds scouring through sand dunes, or streams carving through plateaus define these curved patterns of energy interface.

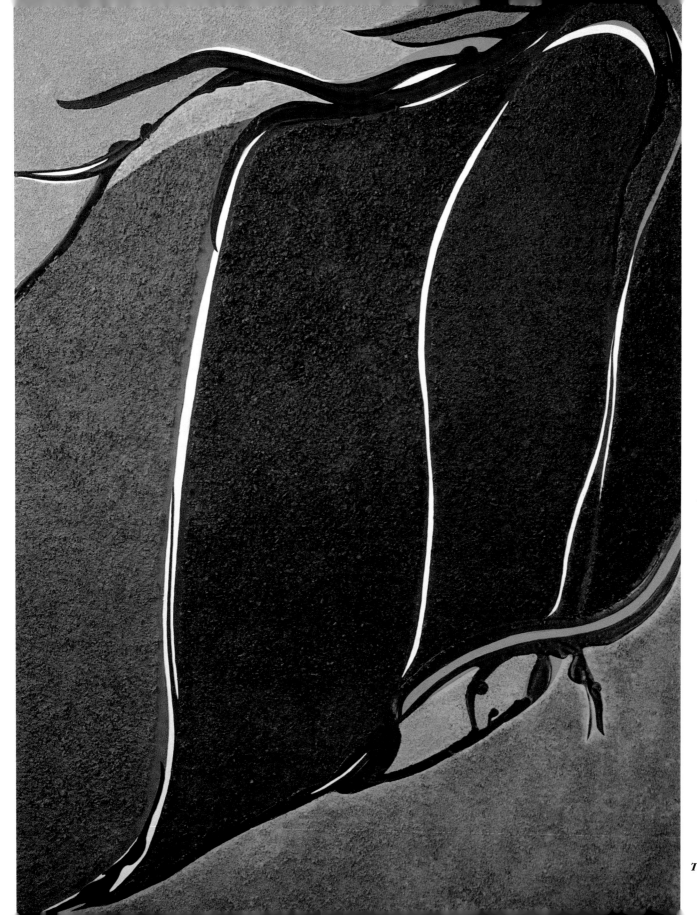

THREE MESAS

LAVA LAKE

Molten lava freezes on contact with air thousands of degrees cooler than itself. The dramatic change also causes contraction and breaks the lava crust into segmented black islands floating on the flowing lava lake. Contrasts of light-dark, chiaroscuro relationships also release light intensity as if from a subterranean furnace. The lines flow amid the black islands and designate the areas of greatest force; their strength determines direction and pattern.

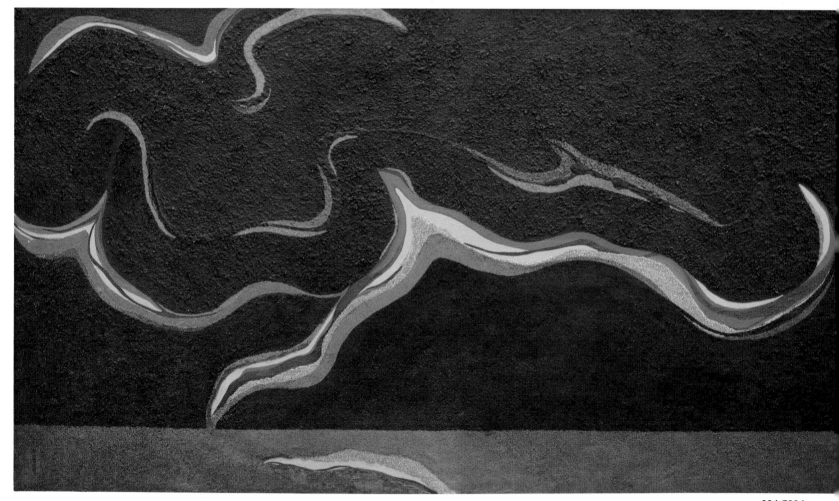

MAGMA

Pattern

And nature must obey necessity.

WILLIAM SHAKESPEARE
JULIUS CAESAR

There are limits on nature. The visual shapes and patterns that we perceive appear to be infinite, but close scrutiny reveals only a few fundamental themes reworked into great variety. These themes are replicated regardless of scale, material, or time.

Our observations seem to tell us of diversity. Rocks and roadrunners, chipmunks and cactus, solar systems and snails: all are different, but similar as well. The serpentine loops of a desert canyon resemble the trail of a sidewinder, the cracks which form in the mud of a drying desert arroyo look like the interconnecting plates of a desert tortoise shell, the branching of a tree seems to copy the branching of the tributaries of a desert wash eroding into a hill of soft mud.

Nature disguises her forms by clothing them in variety, but the same basic patterns prevail. The same players play different roles in different costumes. Hexagons inhabit two-dimensional space but do not enclose the third dimension. Pentagons define the pattern for many flowers but not for crystals. There are seven crystal systems to encompass all the materials of the earth, not eight. Five regular polyhedrons enclose space, not six. Explosions direct concentrated mass outward in space, whether petals of a daisy or rocks from a volcanic explosion. Spirals or meanders are the most efficient means of connecting a uniform scatter of points. A stream meanders because by that method, given enough time, it will move every grain of sand in its plain while expending the smallest possible amount of energy.

There are also rigid physical constraints upon the size of things. Gravity controls the size to which forms can grow. Since area increases arithmetically and volume expands geometrically, the size and shape of objects do not enlarge or contract uniformly. Although the constraints are rigorous, great variety can occur within the limits. The rules dictate a relatedness of purpose and a constancy of design that are aesthetically pleasing and remind us of the unity of the natural world. Plants, rocks, space, dust, liquids, and solids all play the game and abide by the fundamental rules. The infinitely varied structures of natural shapes and forms that have evolved through time are the basic facts of our existence.

Through microscopic or telescopic investigation, new details and perspectives of nature's abstractions come into focus. The smallest unexpected incidents boggle the mind and transform themselves to greatness. The revelations of these visual surprises of unique compositional arrangements suggest mysteries analogous to those discovered through the creativity of the artist. The artist in search of his own nature actualizes unseen mysteries and patterns from within himself. The need to create moves as a force similar to the external evolution of the natural world.

Man and nature move within the limits of existing elements (of which both are made), within what has already been created and continues to undergo change. The artist may intuitively and coincidentally develop abstract motifs that already exist in nature: colors, shapes, textures, and patterns, which resemble rocks, strata, plants, anatomical structures, infinite arrangements of space and structure. Arrangements are unique if the artist is truly creative, yet these patterns are archetypically familiar because their roots are in nature. In many ways the artist is only a vehicle for the transference of energy. The common denominators of life manifest themselves through similar components and molecular movements.

Small creatures
With twenty million heartbeats
How few summers will intermingle
Leaf patterns on the forest's terrain

FRANCISCAN

The apparent random design of the material world is a thinly veiled disguise veneering a rigid set of patterns that control the shapes of rocks, plants, and animals. The nature of the internal atomic structure and the patterns that achieve completion with the least effort combine to control the configurations and fractures in sandstone.

Shifts in position yield changing perspectives of desert forms. In and out relationships exist in spatial fields from distant views to surface ones, and form pictorial patterns. Shapes recede and advance to enliven a breathing space.

DESERT SPACE

Fluidity and rhythmic contours are born into the freedom and flight of clouds, branches, and drying earth, creating curvilinear patterns moving simultaneously in all directions as a covey of birds whose wings crisscross in all directions. The drying of desert mud creates contraction in the sediment. Since upper layers dry first, they contract and cause a wrinkling or curling. Horizontal layers bend upward into space in the intensity of the hot desert sun.

SUDDENLY THEY TAKE WING

CALVILLE WASH

Far up a remote desert wash, the tilted remnants of a fifteen million-year-old dry lake lie eroding in the sun. Borate crystals formed in the drying mud and created characteristic spherical forms. The present erosive forces peel off the ancient mud layers, exposing the subsurfaces. Simultaneously there exists a sense of gravity and antigravitational contrast, weight and buoyancy. Large and small forms exist harmoniously in patterns united within parallel structures. Color comes through the transparent glazes of parallel areas, which act as the source and control of the sensuous spherical forms.

HAPPINESS

Texture

The sense of space built up by touch is not static. It has to do with movement over and around surfaces.

JUDITH AND HERBERT KOHL
THE VIEW FROM THE OAK

Texture to a geologist is the size, shape, and arrangement of the components of a rock rather than merely its surface expression. These properties are essentially geometrical. They may exhibit a scalar property with magnitude but no direction, or they may have a vectorial property with both magnitude and direction. The scalar properties directly reflect the degree of maturity. Particles, eroded from outcrops, transported great distances, become rounded and smaller. Large angular fragments speak of short distances traveled and relative immaturity. The vectorial properties are usually acquired at the time of deposition of the rock fragments. Gravitational and magnetic forces arrange the particles into directional patterns of least resistance.

Intuitively, as well as intellectually, we recognize the importance of rock texture as a clue to the history of the rock. Mature rocks with rounded particles, similar in composition and small in grain size, appear old. These are rocks with experience—rough edges are worn smooth and there is a uniformity of appearance. The past determines the present character.

Much of the desert surface is immature. As a reflection of the recent uplift of our western mountains, the desert is scattered with large rock fragments of great variety and form. The desert is unmodified and unsorted. The texture speaks of youth, of the promise of change.

Gravity is the mover of the earth. Stripped of plants or old eroded sediment, the desert surface portrays the power and omnipresence of gravity, which holds the fragments of the earth together and prevents them from spinning off into the void. Gravity also disintegrates uplifted rock. Any rock above the deep ocean floor is attacked, destroyed, and moved fragment by fragment to the sea. Desert rocks will inevitably submit to this assault from gravitational forces. Psychologically we know this when we walk the desert, and it makes the land pulse with freshness and excitement.

Textures are also inherent in the materials the artist uses. These materials, no matter how altered or modified, are extensions of the materials of the earth—and they behave essentially like the earth's surface. The artist, in this way, is linked to the earth and interacts with it, as well as with the technological processes which transform, manufacture, and distribute the products necessary to his trade.

Many things create the texture of surfaces: rough and smooth papers, the weave and weight of canvas, viscosity of pigment, the grain of wood, the matrix of stone, the nature of synthetic materials. All are available for exploration, each with an intrinsic quality to be respected, interpreted, manipulated. The surface treatment of an art work is the unfolding story of its development, of the concepts and techniques used by the artist. The medium, ground, and method of application determine the textural nature and spatial activity of the surface, making it more tangible and dynamic. The microstructures are unified to enliven the total statement. Texture increases tension and movement and allows a wider range of contrast and personal expression. Light absorption and reflection are intensified and controlled by the nature of the medium or through the rendering of textural illusions developed out of the medium itself. Simulated details that suggest an equivalent photographic representation often deceive the viewer. On a two-dimensional plane, multiple repetitious lines or strokes may create the feeling of rough textural qualities, and uniform applications may show the soft, smooth characteristics of blending relationships.

We take for granted everyday aspects in our environment—the sinewy veins of a leaf, the velvet petals of a rose, the coarse complexity of bark—forgetting to touch, to reexamine, to consider origin, development, and adaptation, to consider the story of the total configuration as evidenced in textural surfaces. Most desert plants do not invite our touch. To the contrary, they warn and repel, excite our vision and wonder. The teleological purpose of their surfaces is their protection and survival.

Awareness, increased by touch (pain, coolness, warmth, sensuousness) and by visual contrasts, enlarges the dimensions of the senses and takes us closer to the fulfillment of the desire to know things and to have confidence in their solidity, temperature, and substantiality. Textural concerns and contrasts are as alive as the world around us.

One is thorny
Sullen but rough to touch
Many are composed here
A microcosm of shapes

Joy to all surfaces
Submerged in each
It's a tingling sensation
To be
Thin and sharp
Round and soft
Hard and weak
Monumental

Alive

POTOSI ORE

Texture is derived from the extreme countermovements of color and particles, which together induce an implosion-explosion cycle reaching a climax of visual and auditory stimuli.

NUN SOFIT #2

There are forces which control all motion in the universe. The movement of seemingly random flows of lava is arranged by these forces. From chaos comes direction. The contents of a channel formed by the fluidity of motion deposit a richness of pattern and texture. Sand and sawdust with pigment achieve earth textures which build, erode, and suggest continuity and changing forms.

LAVA TUBE

NATURE LIVES IN
MOTION

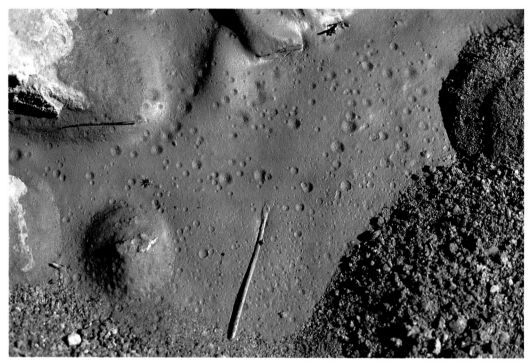

RAINDROPS

A spontaneous event can stamp its mark on a surface that may be preserved for millennia. Raindrops imprinting mud after a desert storm leave impressions to preserve a capricious moment in time. The suggestion of form is developed by unpremeditated, unpredictable movements, by emotions, instincts, buried feelings, even by the weather.

Sensuousness

It seemed as if her heart in her breast were a second unconquerable sun, into the glow and creative strength of which he plunged further and further.

D.H. LAWRENCE
WOMEN IN LOVE

The landscapes of our anatomy resound with color and forms of art and nature, and the sensuous aspects of the desert readily suggest our own forms. Shapes are seen in round, eroded configurations that remind us of male and female bodies. Defiant pinnacles pierce the sky in contrast to supple breast-like mounds and hills. Our bodies rest and touch the earth while heat exudes from the surface skin of the rocks to warm us. Our aging skin parallels the wrinkles, furrows, and dehydrated mud-cracked patterns of the earth.

Fertile fields contrast with glistening plains of spewn lava where sturdy plants can be found pushing their way from beneath the lava surface to air and life. A natural cleavage high on a craggy precipice has a mature, substantial tree or cactus firmly rooted and flourishing. The womb is entered in narrow deep dark canyons and arroyos where passage leads to rebirth and light.

The palette is promise. Inflammable color is life-giving. Vivid crimson hues burst next to lush greens. Sumptuous pigment and spectral colors stir excitement and pleasure. The yellows, golds, umbers, and reds in Rembrandt's paintings delight our aesthetic eye and increase our empathy for the human condition. One feels the love and wonder of light in each brush stroke of the water lilies painted by Monet. One bathes in the glow of atmospheric light created by the Impressionist painters. Van Gogh's energetically applied impasto pigments awaken passions and affirm life. The odors and textures of paint and canvas linger, stimulate, and involve our other senses. Appealing compositional shapes and forms arouse our deepest emotions.

We are kindled by colors, the sun, wind. Water movement, wind, and light enter a pulsating relationship. Making love on the sand, covered by the warmth of the sun and touched by a gentle breeze, near a timeless flowing river, is an exquisite oneness with nature. Passions build with the violent turbulence of rapids. The desert is a beckoning lover, conceiving, transforming, transmitting life energy and force. The richness of our external natural world and the lasting images of great works of art enlarge our senses and cultivate our humanity.

My heart in your stream
Caressed by water's flow
My arms and hands
The rhythmic willows of the wind
My body your veil of warmth
A pool of iridescent silk
In summer stillness

One with you while
Birds sing private songs
And love against the sky

MID HILLS

The natural and inner worlds are the sources from which the artist derives ideas and inspiration. Rock, light, shadow, and texture are translated into the curves of sensuous bodies, just as human forms are translated into aspects of the land.

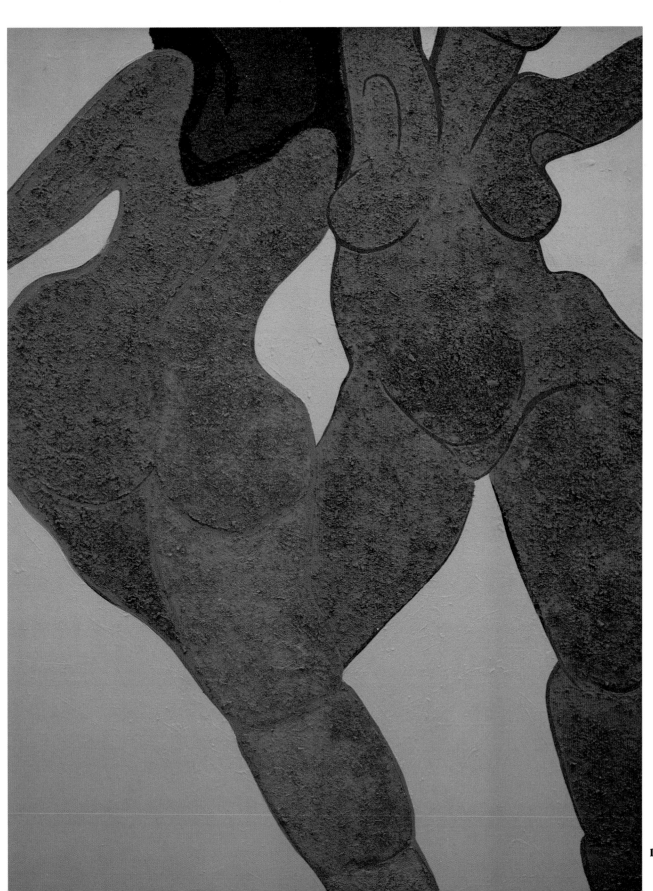

DANCE ETERNAL

WETHERILL CANYON

Contour lines flow to build the solid, sensuous volumes of the female form which readily merge with the topography of the earth. The transition from animate to inanimate flows unimpeded as light and shadow luxuriously caress, reflect, and encompass the voluptuous, corporeal warmth of earthbound rocks.

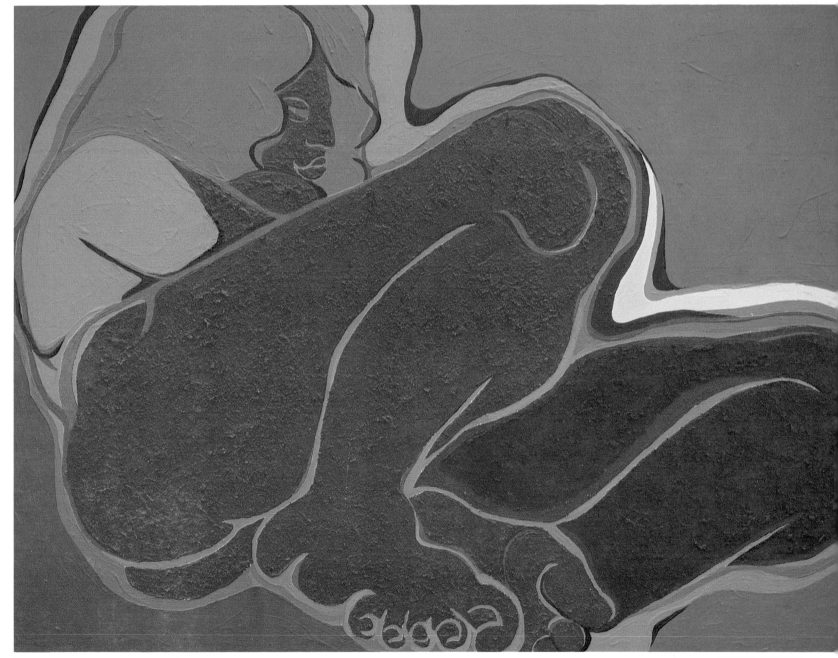

TRANQUILITY

RAVEN

Flight is a sensuous experience. Flying in, under, and around masses, planes, rocks, and branches without collision—defying, piercing, and embracing space—is a thrilling identification with all winged creatures. The complementaries of red and green suggest a totality of light which makes a mystical impression as an afterimage on the eye's retina—an illusive memory of a raven's flight. Time and motion are intimately related. The fixity of a limestone cliff contrasts sharply with the fluid black slash of raven wings. Both are dynamic, undergoing rapid change. But for each there ticks a different clock.

THE RAVEN FLIES

METKATAMIBA

The vertical penetration of an eroding desert arroyo exposes the horizontality of geological layers. The vertical and horizontal merge along the curvilinear open space of the wash. Few environments have greater appeal for an exploration through the sinuous slice of time-space. One remembers the factors that sunder, crumble, alter, and shape strong rhythmic channels and transport matter to new destinations. The cut contoured layers reveal the mystery of birth, opening like a womb to expose their history. These eternal rhythmic forces are expressed in nature and in the natural rhythms of our own existence.

ARROYO

Silence and Sound

QUIET UNTIL THE THAW

*Her name tells of how
it was with her*

*The truth is, she did not speak
in winter . . .*

SWAMPY CREE NAMING STORIES
BORN TYING KNOTS

The individual in search of meaning retreats in solitude to heighten his spiritual understanding. The unspoken is esteemed, and thus each word uttered is imporant and clearly heard. Soundless space invites contemplation and careful observation; it appears larger.

The desert is silent, therefore every sound has significance. The most minute utterance of a bird is magnified and carried over distances, while we marvel, in a trance-like state, at the open winged hawk or raven silently sailing on the currents of the wind. Time is slowed and unlocked with flight, and the freedom of motion exalts and releases secret longings from deep within ourselves.

Rocks and flowers delight in each other and shadows dance in forms never seen before in the darkness of a cave, the heart of a painting. Colors and forms can quietly interpenetrate, or clash and reverberate with deafening proportions. Diagonals increase the dynamics of volume and speed, coexisting with more restful horizontals. The hushed submission of a gargantuan object at gravitational rest is as comfortable and reserved as a pebble nestling near a stream.

The rapidly approaching flash flood, first heard as a mysterious hum resounding dim primordial beginnings, arrives with terrifying thunderous power. Sounds fly freely to shrink distances that visually appear infinite. Yet sight can exceed hearing as well, creating the duality of sound swallowing space and sight anticipating sound. On tranquil, out-of-the-way paths, one's own heartbeat is heard. The wind slipping through plant life, around rocks, cliffs, and down canyons, sings, moans, whispers and screams its wind song. A swift snake and the swallow's dive are heard. The heat waves rising from the rocks seem to emanate audible notes. Life not usually apparent reaches out for attention and calls quietly for an audience.

Consumed by bizarre forms
Through sloping layers of time
With glassy skin fractures
A compressed easy canyon
Offers me myself

The end of my search—
Where a small lizard pauses
And takes me into consideration
In a gift of silence

SUN DOG

Refraction of sunlight through cirrus cloud ice crystals spotlights the spectrum at precise points or arcs in the sky. When the light rays focus on a single wisp of cloud, the rainbow hues mark a brilliant point in the somber sky. The refraction of light plays with clouds, moving our imaginations into a hypnotic trance. Lost in movement, erasing our self-importance, the silence of space releases a memory of all beginnings and connections.

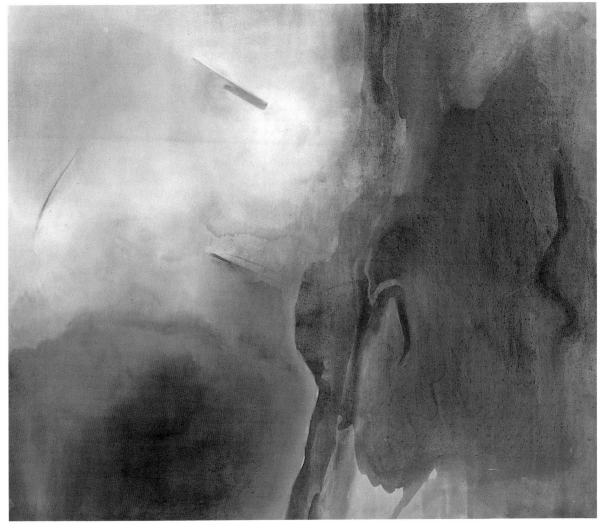

MEMORY

SANAP PLATEAU

The largeness of the land swallows sound. Here in the vast space and distance, the eyes far outreach the ears. Panoramas unfold from plateau to plateau, and only desert thunder can fill the void. Vision predominates. Horizontal overlapping planes suggest a realm of calm and quiet only subtly interrupted by distant underlying movements, rhythmically suggestive of life and atmospheric change. The aerial perspective is illuminated by light made more significant by varying angles of the sun and the oncoming blues of night.

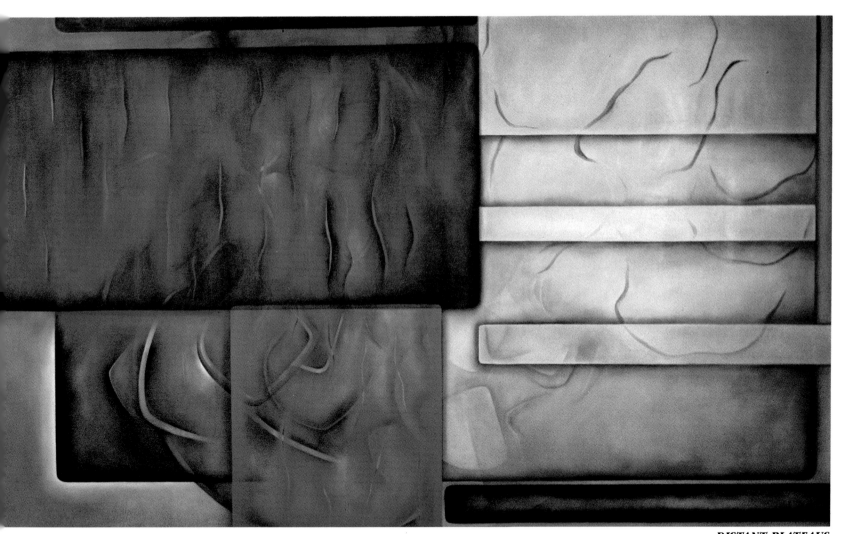

DISTANT PLATEAUS

CLEAR CREEK

The acoustics of a desert canyon magnify sound. Noise in the enclosed space becomes intensified reality. Each footfall crunches against rock. The tremulous descending whistles of a canyon wren and the excited squawking of the magpie echo from wall to wall.

Repeating lines, with electric white edges, reverberate like harp strings and fill the atmosphere with sounds that transform into spectral color nuances. Colors and sounds fuse and resound with time into distance and into the silence of space. Desert silence dominates the land.

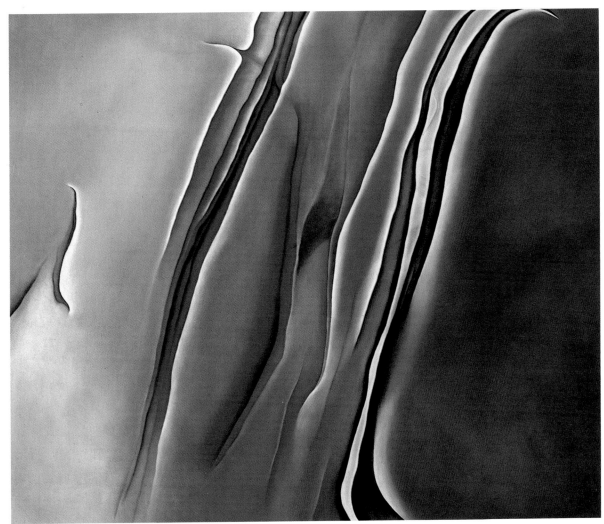

CANYON ECHOES

Notes on the Illustrations

Paintings and Reliefs

Photographs

Rita Deanin Abbey is a Professor of Art in Drawing and Painting at the University of Nevada, Las Vegas. She has had over forty one-woman exhibitions, and her paintings are in museums and private collections. A previous book, *Rivertrip* (Northland Press, 1977), contains her narrative verse and twenty-five color reproductions of drawings and watercolors.

G. William Fiero is a Professor of Geology at the University of Nevada, Las Vegas, and was formally an exploration geologist for Texaco, Inc. He has traveled over most of the world doing geological research and conducting field trips. His observations and scholarly articles have appeared in many professional publications.